Praise for *Show & Tell in a Nu...* **YO-DJP-582**

"Wonderful writer's tool. I could not believe the amount of scenes Jessica managed to create with such flair and intensity. The tone of each was so very different. I have never seen such obvious yet beautiful examples of showing. As an editor, I look forward to recommending this book to my authors. It has the ability to broaden a writer's horizon, not just in showing, but in the tone and temper used." ~Amie McCracken, writer & editor

"A must-have for every writer. Writers are frequently instructed to "show, not tell", but before we can follow that advice, we first have to understand it. Bell's brilliant nuts-and-bolts examples provide just what every writer needs to not only understand the concept, but to implement it. Know why? She doesn't just tell us about this concept ... she shows us. Kinda fitting, dontcha think?" ~Susan Flett Swiderski, author of *Hot Flashes & Cold Lemonade*

"I found lots of helpful writing tips and examples in this book. I'd recommend it to all new writers, especially students trying to hone their fiction writing skills." ~A. K. Borenstadt, writer

Praise for *Adverbs & Clichés in a Nutshell:*

"I love the structure of this book. Its quick and to-the-point examples are genius and so easy to follow, very user-friendly. Throughout her examples, Bell challenges the writer to see these flaws in his/her writing, but not to panic. She points out they are easy pitfalls for any writer. Even the most seasoned of writers must be reminded from time to time about certain aspects of their writing: i.e., thus the need for editors. This is a MUST HAVE for any writer's craft arsenal, along with its companion—Book I, *Show & Tell in a Nutshell: Demonstrated Transitions from Telling to Showing*. It would also be a fabulous gift for any high school or college student." ~Sheri Larsen, children's literature author

"The examples selected by the author encompass most adverbs and clichés in use. Her suggestions/alternatives are simply brilliant, even poetic in some cases. I wish I could describe things in such a beautiful and clever way like her! But that's why I bought this book. I'm motivated enough to pimp my prose now! I definitely recommend it." ~Aline Lerner, writer

Praise for *The Six Senses in a Nutshell*:

"I'm a big fan of the 'In a Nutshell' series, and *The Six Senses In a Nutshell* is an excellent addition. If you have trouble including sensory detail in your prose, this handy little guide of exercises will help bring your writing to life! Like the rest of the series, these guides work best if you actually do the exercises. Only then will you discover your own writing style and voice. I found that working through the guide helped me pinpoint the areas in my own novel that lacked vivid setting and description. It's so hard to edit your own work, but Jessica Bell's guides have been invaluable for teaching me the fine art of self-editing and revision. I highly recommend this guide as a standalone for those wanting to improve the use of senses in their writing, but I believe the guides work best in conjunction with one another. They also make great gifts for writers, especially those in your critique group!" ~Angela Mackintosh, Founder/CEO at WOW! Women On Writing

"In each Nutshell guide, Jessica Bell provides a focused and effective master class on a single aspect of the writer's craft. To read each book feels like taking a personal tutorial, with expert advice couched in friendly, supportive terms and reinforced by carefully planned exercises. A highly recommended source of practical help to refine any author's writing skills." ~Debbie Young, author of *Sell Your Books* and editor of The Alliance of Independent Authors Self-Publishing Advice Blog.

WRITING IN
A NUTSHELL

Writing Workshops to Improve Your Craft

jessica bell

Vine Leaves Press
Melbourne, Vic, Australia

Writing in a Nutshell:
Writing Workshops to Improve Your Craft

Copyright © 2014 Jessica Bell
All rights reserved.

ISBN-10: 098759317X
ISBN-13: 978-0-9875931-7-7

Published by Vine Leaves Press, 2014
Melbourne, Vic, Australia

A CIP catalogue record for this book is available from the National
Library of Australia

This is the all-in-one edition of the three "Writing in a Nutshell"
workbooks: *Show & Tell in a Nutshell: Demonstrated Transitions from Telling to
Showing*; *Adverbs & Clichés in a Nutshell: Demonstrated Subversions of Adverbs
& Clichés into Gourmet Imagery*; and *The Six Senses in a Nutshell: Demonstrated
Transitions from Bleak to Bold Narrative*.

Cover design by Jessica Bell

ABOUT THE AUTHOR

If Jessica Bell could choose only one creative mentor, she'd give the role to Euterpe, the Greek muse of music and lyrics. This is not only because she currently resides in Athens, Greece, but because of her life as a thirty-something Australian-native contemporary fiction author, poet and singer/songwriter/guitarist, whose literary inspiration often stems from songs she's written.

Jessica is the Co-Publishing Editor of *Vine Leaves Literary Journal* and the director of the Homeric Writers' Retreat & Workshop on the Greek island of Ithaca. She makes a living as a writer/editor for English Language Teaching Publishers worldwide, such as Pearson Education, HarperCollins, MacMillan Education, Education First and Cengage Learning.

Visit her website: **www.jessicabellauthor.com**

ALSO BY JESSICA BELL

Novels
Bitter Like Orange Peel
The Book
String Bridge

Short Fiction
muted: a short story in verse
The Hum of Sin Against Skin

Poetry Collections
Fabric
Twisted Velvet Chains

Non-Fiction
Show & Tell in a Nutshell: Demonstrated Transitions from
Telling to Showing (Writing in a Nutshell Series, Book 1)

Adverbs & Clichés in a Nutshell: Demonstrated Subversions
of Adverbs & Clichés Into Gourmet Imagery (Writing in a
Nutshell Series, Book 2)

The Six Senses in a Nutshell: Demonstrated Transitions from
Bleak to Bold Narrative (Writing in a Nutshell Series, Book 3)

Compiled & Edited
The Best of Vine Leaves Literary Journal 2012
The Best of Vine Leaves Literary Journal 2013
Indiestructible: Inspiring Stories from the Publishing Jungle

WRITING IN A NUTSHELL

Writing Workshops to Improve Your Craft

jessica bell

NOTE FROM THE AUTHOR

In order to get the most out of these workshops, please be sure to read the introduction in each separate book before reading the demonstrated transitions. They include important instructions on how to read, analyze, and exploit each demonstrated transition to your advantage. There are also fifteen **bonus writing exercises** at the end of this all-in-one edition, that are not in the individual books. Enjoy!

CONTENTS

FOREWORD

In *Bird by Bird*, Anne Lamott says a writer needs to focus on short assignments to avoid feeling overwhelmed. She refers to the one-inch picture frame on her desk and how it reminds her to focus on bite-sized pieces of the whole story. If you focus on one small thing at a time, the story will eventually come together to create a whole. The same applies to learning writing craft. If writers focus on one aspect of the craft at a time, the process will seem less daunting, and piece by piece, it will come together.

With more than ten years' experience as an editor and writer of English Language Teaching (ELT) materials for various ELT publishers worldwide, I know that "breaking down" language into smaller focus areas is an effective learning method. After much experimentation on myself, and volunteer aspiring writers, I discovered it is extremely effective with creative writing too. And so the *Writing in a Nutshell Series* was born.

This book is the all-in-one edition of the three *Writing in a Nutshell* workbooks: *Show & Tell in a Nutshell: Demonstrated Transitions from Telling to Showing*; *Adverbs & Clichés in a Nutshell: Demonstrated Subversions of Adverbs & Clichés into Gourmet Imagery*; and *The Six Senses in a Nutshell: Demonstrated Transitions from Bleak to Bold Narrative*.

In each book, I guide you through a variety of "before" and "after" writing examples demonstrating the transition from weak to strong writing, and encourage you to follow my example through clear and simple self-teaching steps.

Not only is this all-in-one workbook an excellent addition to any creative writing course, but also a great primary learning tool for aspiring writers. Even if you're an established writer, the exercises in this book will keep you at the top of your game.

What are you waiting for? Getting cracking on improving your writing craft!

Jessica Bell

BOOK #1

Show & Tell in a Nutshell
Demonstrated Transitions from Telling to Showing

BOOK #1 CONTENTS

INTRODUCTION

When I first started to write fiction and send my manuscripts out for feedback, the first and most frequent thing my readers said was SHOW, DON'T TELL.

In theory, I understood what SHOW, DON'T TELL meant. But it was almost impossible for me to put it into practice after comments such as, "Why don't you show your character sitting in a café getting frustrated with her friend? I'd really like to see that happening, rather than just being told it's happening. It would give us a lot more insight into their characters."

Okay. So how do I go about that? I'm not sure I understand how you can't see it happening when I'm telling you it's happening. What's the difference?

I never truly understood the difference until I'd accomplished it by accident one day. My motivation was that I needed to increase the word count in one of my manuscripts. I had a 60,000 word novel that needed 80,000–100,000 before I could submit it to agents.

I combed through my manuscript, marking scenes I thought I could expand. By the time I'd finished reworking the first scene, the concept clicked. I finally understood what all the fuss was about. My writing had become cinematic, it had movement, my characters were three dimensional and I didn't even have to mention their personality traits because I was showing them. But above all, my writing evoked emotion. This is what successful showing does. It uses the five senses (and sixth) to evoke an emotional response from your reader without telling them how you want them to feel. Simply put, does me saying Hilary felt scared make you feel scared? Of course not.

Do you get it? Not really? That's why I felt the need to publish this little book. To SHOW YOU, how to SHOW, INSTEAD OF TELL. It's one resource I craved and couldn't find during the early years. I needed real examples that clearly demonstrated the transition from telling to showing, in a small, concise, non-threatening, non-overwhelming format. Something I could dip into without getting lost in the jungle of technical jargon that I never really understood until I Googled my fingertips into flames. I learned better by example. By physically doing and reworking, making mistakes and fixing them through trial and error.

No matter how entertaining, diverse, concise, or detailed, a writing craft book is, it's not going to work magic on you, it's not going to suddenly make you a brilliant writer simply by reading it. You need to use what you read and learn in your own writing. Because that's when you have those AHA moments. That's when it really sticks.

By analyzing the sixteen scenes in this book, you will clearly see how to transition telling into showing through a variety of situations, emotions, and characteristics.

I suggest you follow these steps:

Step one: For the first read-through, read both the "telling" and "showing" scenes in their entirety without stopping, to grasp a general feel for them.

Step two: For the second read-through, identify the "telling" words/phrases that are shown in the reworked piece.

Step three: For the third read-through, identify *how* those "telling" words/phrases are shown, i.e., what actions/behaviour are used instead.

Step four: For the fourth and final read through, brainstorm your own ways of depicting the listed attributes from the scene, and try your hand at writing your own "showing" example of my "telling" example.

Note: You will find these attributes listed in the Contents, the Index of Attributes, and at the beginning of each scene for your convenience.

In this print edition, I have provided some blank lined pages at the back of the book for you to jot down your notes and ideas as you read.

Three short writing prompts are also provided.

Please note: *It's not essential to show every single scene. Sometimes you do need some telling in order to move the necessary, but not so important moments, forward. You'll discover the appropriate balance, and a more sophisticated way of telling, with lots of reading and writing practice.*

Have fun and happy showing!

SCENE 1

amazing view • awe • (feel) hot • relief • (feel) tired

Telling

Sandy stood at the foot of the Egyptian Pyramids. Though she was hot, tired and sore, she was awestruck by the amazing view and felt a sense of relief. Finally, she'd made it.

Showing

Sweat ran between Sandy's breasts and the soles of her feet burned from the two hour trek across the desert. Even though her shoulders ached from carrying her heavy rucksack, and her nose stung from the dry heat, it didn't matter. She was standing right in front of something she'd been waiting to see her whole life. The Pyramids of Giza glistened through heat waves as if extracting all her pain. Sandy looked up, shielded her eyes from the sun, refused to break her stare. She stood, jaw agape, wondering how she'd kept away for so long.

SCENE 2

boredom • living conditions • mess

Telling

Neli lives in a loft with her cat. It's a mess, but she can't ever be bothered cleaning it. She is so bored today. She tries to pass the time by reading a magazine, but she's not interested in it. So she turns on the TV, but there's nothing on that she wants to watch either.

Showing

Neli stares at the dusty clock, wondering if it's possible for the hands to slow down every time she looks at them. She grabs the nearest magazine off the coffee table and flicks through the pages like a robot, staring at the oil stain on her thigh. She clicks her tongue, throws the magazine on the sofa, and searches her loft for the remote control. After upending piles of clothes and moldy dishes, she finds it in the cat's bed, grabs it, blows off some grey feline hair and switches on the TV. Neli glares at it, changes channels a few times, groans, then flicks it off again.

SCENE 3

anger • challenge • confidence • fight

Telling

Chuck, a pimply bully, threw a basketball at Gary's head in anger. Gary caught it without even looking. Chuck seemed to be annoyed by his confidence, so Gary decided to challenge him to a few basketball tricks in the school yard, instead of getting mixed up in a fight.

Showing

"Watch your mouth, you dick!" Chuck hurled the basketball at Gary's head. Gary caught it with one hand, maintaining his stare toward the pock marks that scarred Chuck's pink face. Chuck stepped forward. Cocked his fist. But with a quick flick of his wrist, Gary engaged the basketball into a rapid spin, forefinger taut, and winked, "You game to take this outside, dude?"

SCENE 4

disgust • dizziness

Telling

When Darrel got home from the supermarket there was a dirty homeless man sitting on his doorstep. As Darrel tried to get inside, the man said and did some disgusting things that freaked Darrel out. He gently kicked the homeless man aside, but before he knew it, the guy had thrown up on Darrel's feet! Of course, Darrel left his shoes on his doorstep. But it was no good. The smell of the vomit and the shock of the situation made him dizzy, and when he finally got inside, he ended up throwing up on his own feet too.

Showing

"Luv, come 'ere so I can give ya tush a squeeze." The man sitting on Darrel's doorstep looked like he'd come straight out of a chimney in Mary Poppins.

Without making eye contact, Darrel turned the key in his front door, grocery bags hooked on his wrist. He hoped to slip past without any fuss, but as soon as he put one foot in the door, the man clutched his ankle, tumbled onto his back and looked up between his legs as if inspecting a woman's crotch. Darrel stepped backward and nudged the old man away with one foot.

What's that smell?

Too late. Darrel's new snake skin shoes were covered in gunk. It resembled mushroom soup.

Oh my God!

Darrel held his breath, kicked off his shoes, jumped inside and slammed the door. He closed his eyes, leaned his back against the wall, and tried to synchronize his breathing as his head spun.

1 hippopotamus, 2 hippopotamus ...
Keep it down. Keep it down!

But he couldn't.

Now he'd have to give the man his socks too.

SCENE 5

flightiness • frustration • (be) in love
• self-importance

Telling

Tamara and Fran are having lunch at a café. They
are seated outdoors. But it seems useless meeting at
all when Fran is so flighty. It's ridiculously frustrating
talking to Fran when she's like this—off in her own
little world. She doesn't even acknowledge what's
being said when Tamara raises her voice! Perhaps
she's in love.

Showing

"Can you pass the salt?" Tamara holds out her
hand.

"Hmm?" Fran hums and looks across the road at
the kids playing Frisbee.

"Hun? The salt." Tamara glances at the kids, screws
up her nose, and contorts her mouth to the left.

"Oh. Right." Fran passes the ketchup.

Tamara groans and reaches across the table for

the salt. As she leans over her plate, her blouse dips into the mayonnaise.

"Crap! I need a serviette." Tamara points at the napkin holder. Francine is resting her chin in her palm, squinting at the sky, giggling to herself.

Christ.

"Fran!" Tamara bangs her fist on the table. Crockery rattles.

Fran's smile fades as she jolts upright. "Huh? What's wrong?"

Tamara stands, scrapes her seat backward, reaches for a serviette, and shakes her head. "I can't count on you for even the simplest of things, can I?"

Francine blinks.

Tamara dips a serviette into her glass of soda and rubs it on her breast. "So. Who's the guy?"

"Tammie?" Francine sighs. "Have you ever wondered why we only see yellow butterflies in this area of town?"

SCENE 6

doubt • handsome • hope • (feel) nervous
• positive thinking • routine

Telling

Handsome Hank has an interview today for a job he really wants. And he's nervous about it. Deep down, he knows he's perfect for the position, but he has a niggling feeling that something isn't going to go as planned. Despite his doubts, Hank goes about his morning routine, trying not to think too much about the day ahead. He must think positively. It's the only way he's going to succeed.

Showing

Hank jerks upright in bed at the sound of his alarm.

He rubs his eyes, stretches his arms and yawns so loud and wide his jaw cracks. He stands. Farts. A sharp pain shoots across his abdomen and his stomach gurgles.

Ugh. Please don't be sick. Not today.

Armed with toast and freshly brewed coffee, he sits at the kitchen table, and opens the morning newspaper. He stares into the center of the feature article until all the words blend together in a kaleidoscopic swirl.

No. Stop it. It will all be fine.

After breakfast, Hank brushes his teeth, admiring his sharp cheek bones and dark features in the bathroom mirror. He smiles and nods. Toothpaste dribbles from the corner of his mouth onto his pale blue tailored shirt.

"Christ!" He spits his toothpaste into the sink. Flecks of pinky foam splash on the mirror. Hank rinses out his mouth, grabs the hand towel off the rod below the sink, and wipes away the sticky mess. The metal rod spins and echoes against the hospital white tiles like a bad omen. For a moment it feels like a pocket of air is stuck in his chest, struggling to find an out.

Hank coughs into a closed fist, smoothes his shirt against his chest, and takes a deep breath. He grins and winks at his reflection.

"You're the man. Go get 'em."

SCENE 7

disappointment • disapproval • disrespect
• indifference • (to) persuade • unhealthy marriage

Telling

Across the road from Kathy and Jack lives a man who doesn't care about the environment. He's always wasting water, and in Kathy's opinion, he should be stopped. She tries to persuade Jack to see her point, and to help her stop the man from being so careless, but all Jack seems to care about is blocking Kathy's voice out with the TV. She hates it when he treats her like this, always ignoring her, disrespecting her. Always making her cry for no reason at all. Their marriage is on the brink of ruin.

Showing

Kathy stood by her living room window with her arms crossed, the lines in her forehead growing deeper with every huff and puff.

"Can you believe this guy rids his driveway of leaves with the hose? Every day?" Kathy threw her arms in the air and shook her head.

Jack shrugged, sat on the couch, switched on the

TV, opened a packet of Oreos.

"I think we should do something about it, don't you? Look at all that fresh water going down the drain."

Silence.

Kathy tsked, stomped over to Jack, and hovered above him with her hands on her hips. Jack looked up mid chew, jaw slightly open.

"Jack? This man has to be stopped." Kathy pointed her arm toward the window so hard her elbow cracked. "Did you know that in Australia they fine you something like 500 dollars if you are caught wasting water?"

Jack groaned, turned up the volume on the TV, and snapped, "Oh for God's sake, Kath, we don't live in Australia, do we? Now move. My show is on."

Kathy's breath caught in her throat. She swallowed, looked at her feet, and quietly left the room when a tear surfaced and trickled down her cheek.

SCENE 8

alcoholism • hangover

Telling

My mother got drunk again last night and passed out on the sofa. She looks like a disgusting street bum and the house smells like vomit and cigarettes.

Showing

I watch a glob of drool vibrate in the corner of my mother's mouth with every breath of air that struggles through her sticky cracked lips. Strands of stiff bleach-blonde hair, clumped together and matted below her ear, look petrified with dried vomit. Her fingers twitch. She has two black nails from when she jammed them in the hinge of the alcohol cabinet door. She groans. One eye opens. A vibrant crystal blue bordered with a yellowy, bloodshot white.

Her eye closes, and she sits up, blindly reaching toward the coffee table for her pack of 50s. It's empty. She scrunches the packet and throws it across the room. It lands between an urn and an empty bottle of gin on the mantle. She opens and closes her mouth in what seems an attempt to rehydrate it, and clicks her tongue, as if tasting something foul.

SCENE 9

anxiety • loneliness • panic attack

Telling

Chloe receives bad news that makes her feel alone and abandoned. She has a panic attack.

Showing

The phone drops from Chloe's hand when the ceiling feels like it's caving in on her head. She grabs the waste paper basket, empties it onto the floor, and scrambles on all fours for the scrunched-up paper bag from yesterday's lunch. She flattens it out, sits up straight, feet tucked under her behind. Her hands shake as she puts the paper bag over her mouth and nose. Holding the sides firmly to her cheeks, she breathes in, vacuuming all the air into her chest.

In. Out. In. Out.

Dizziness takes hold, her stomach a hurricane. She bends over to vomit on the carpet, but all that escapes is air and spit—spit slippery with fear—a fear that she will soon be left with nothing.

Nothing and no one.
Nothing. No one.

SCENE 10

laziness • flu • (feel) miserable

Telling

Ben has man flu. His house has turned into a pig sty and he is acting like a baby because he feels miserable.

Showing

Ben. Sunday morning. Red Sox replay. Background noise. Naked. Cold sweat. Heater taking too long to work. Grabs quilt from couch. Wraps himself in it. Prickly on skin. Especially groin. Itchy scrotum, nostril, big toe. Goes to bedroom. Puts on boxers. The red ones covered in giraffes. Drags toe along carpet. One itch relieved. Wraps himself in quilt again. Returns to kitchen. Scratches bum crack through prickly quilt. Not comfortable. Gets angry at quilt. Throws it at couch. Goes back into bedroom. Puts on tracksuit. Returns to kitchen. Coffee made. Can't remember turning machine on. Farts. Pasta petrified in pot on stove. Smells foul, triggers gag reflex. Covers it with tea towel. Goes back to bed. Wishes he still lived with Mom.

SCENE 11

jealousy • hide feelings • pretense

Telling

I'm so jealous of Gloria's brand new piano. It's so beautiful and I wish it was mine. I don't like Gloria much. I always get the feeling she's only pretending to like me.

Showing

"Why don't you sit down and have a play?" Gloria smirked and stroked the side of her new grand piano. It shined like a glazed cherry tart. I tamed an irrational urge to scratch it with my wedding ring. I shook my dusty cardigan above it instead. Gloria's brow puckered as she ran her sleeve along the keys, her clenched teeth hidden by a civil smile.

SCENE 12

foreplay • lust • physical attraction

Telling

Sam thinks Janet is sexy. She has hardly come through his door when he seduces her.

Showing

Sam wraps his arms around Janet's stomach from behind. Her body slackens in his embrace, her handbag drops to the floor.

He slips his right hand beneath her sweater and runs circles around her navel with his middle finger. He teases the opening of her jeans with the tips of his fingers and bites her ear. The hesitation in Janet's gasp makes his penis twitch and push against his fly.

"Don't you want any music?" Janet whispers.

"You are my music." Sam hooks two fingers into Janet's left jean pocket and pulls her toward the couch.

SCENE 13

(feel) embarrassed • naivety • realization

Telling

Despite her recent grounding, Helen let Nina out of her sight to pay a few bills at the mall. Naively, Helen believed that Nina's motives were pure, and that she was only trying to help out. But Gordon points out that the only reason Nina is being so kind is so she can see her no-good boyfriend. Helen realizes that Gordon is right and feels a little embarrassed.

Showing

"Where's Nina?" Gordon scraped his leftover bacon into the dog's bowl.

"She's gone to pay our bills, can you believe it?"

"Helen ... since when is she so helpful?"

"Don't be so cynical. She's probably just realizing she needs to pull her weight around here more. Great, hey?" Helen put the last of the dry dishes away and leaned her hip against the counter. She winked and crossed her arms over her chest with a satisfied sigh.

"You can't be serious." Gordon put his bowl in the sink and rubbed his hands on his thighs.

"Why wouldn't I be?"

"We just grounded her. Yesterday."

"So?"

"We told her she wasn't allowed to see Con anymore?"

"And?"

"Where does Con work?"

Helen shrugged, "The ma—," she said, then dropped her head into her hands. "Oh."

SCENE 14

clothing • suicide

Telling

Karin commits suicide in the beautiful gothic dress she wore for her debut performance, back before she hated her life.

Showing

Karin fingers the raw blue-grey tulle and black crow feathers of her skirt, and remembers the day she performed in it for the very first time, before the horrors of reality surfaced, and then suffocated her with sadness.

She steps backward, into the river, moving down a slipway now overgrown with slick moss. As the water inches up her body, the skirt of her dress floats around her thighs like lily pads, then flicks up around her taut nipples—an inverted umbrella in wind.

The water soaks through the fabric, staining it with the decomposing fears of those who have already succumbed to the river's call, and she releases her body into darkness, freeing herself from her heavy flesh.

SCENE 15

(be) accommodating • idiosyncrasies • (be) kind
• new relationship

Telling

Jon and Jill have just moved in together. Jill is finding it a little bit difficult to get used to Jon's idiosyncrasies, but it seems that Jon is settling in just fine. He's such a sweet and quirky guy, always eager to do whatever makes Jill happy. He's definitely got that going for him.

Showing

Jon butters his raisin toast, licks the knife and balances it on the edge of the microwave.

"Why can't you just put it in the sink?" Jill bites into her banana muffin to stunt her nag reflex.

Jon shrugs, "Because I'll probably use it again."

This new living together thing better not be the death of me, Jill thinks.

"If you really do plan to use it again, can you actually … you know, use it again?"

Damn. You just can't help yourself can you?

"Whaddaya mean?" Jon furrows his brow.

Jill sighs.

Just say it.

"Well, yesterday I found used butter knives on the edge of the coffee table, on top of the coffee maker, on your bedside table, on your desk, balanced on top of the stapler, and on the side of the bathroom sink so close to the edge I have no idea how you got it to stay there." Jill laughs, hoping to sound like she's making fun rather than pestering. "Were you planning to reuse all of them?"

Jon scoffs, takes the knife off the microwave and puts it in the sink. He kisses Jill on the forehead and says, "I guess you got me."

SCENE 16

sarcasm • tantrum • (be) tense

Telling

It's Thanksgiving and we're expecting family to knock on the door at any minute. But as of right now, there's not much to do besides wait. So I read. But my uptight sister thinks I'm being lazy and confiscates my book. When I refuse to get up she throws a tantrum. This is going to be the worst Thanksgiving ever.

Showing

Liz purses her lips and snatches the book from my hands.

"You're not going to read today." She tucks my book under her arm. "Mom and Dad are coming. And you know how they are."

"But there's nothing do to."

"Doesn't matter. Get up." Liz yanks the tea towel off her shoulder and flicks my legs with it.

"Ouch! They're not even here yet!"

"They will be soon. And the turkey's almost done."

"Well, I'll read 'til they come or when the timer starts buzzing. Now gimme my book back. Please." I hold out my hand. Liz squints and shakes her head.

"Will you just chill out?" I squeal. "What's the big deal?"

"Can you just get up? I will not have you ruin this day for me. It has to be perfect."

"I promise I will stop reading the instant someone walks in the door. Okay?"

Liz growls, stamps her feet like a two-year-old who's been denied candy, and hurls my book across the room. It hits the wall and drops to the floor like a dead animal.

Thanksgiving is going to be freakin' excellent.

NOW IT'S YOUR TURN

1. Change the following from telling to showing:

Claudia has never felt so ill and miserable in her entire life. And she doesn't have anyone to look after her. Her parents died a couple of years ago. And it doesn't seem to be getting easier. It just sort of … comes in waves. There are good days, of course. But she misses them so much.

2. Write a scene demonstrating these attributes:

(be) confused
(feel) flattered
generosity

3. Now extend one or more of the showing scenes in this book.

BOOK #2

Adverbs & Clichés in a Nutshell

Demonstrated Subversions of Adverbs & Clichés into Gourmet Imagery

BOOK #2 CONTENTS

INTRODUCTION

Writers constantly have rules thrown at them left, right, and center. *Show, don't tell! Stop using so many dialogue tags! More sensory detail! More tension! Speed up the pace!* Yada yada yada … it can become overwhelming, yes? I used to feel overwhelmed by it all too. In fact, I still do sometimes. It's hard enough to get the words on the page, let alone consider *how* to put them there.

My own struggles have led me to write this series of pocket-sized writing guides. So you can learn to hone your craft in bite-sized, manageable pieces. But please keep in mind, their purpose is to inspire you to become better at your craft. To teach you how to grow as a writer. They will not tell you how to write. They will not preach writing rules and styles to you. But they will help you realize that you can, little by little, end up with a work of fiction as unique as your own soul (whether you regard your soul as a spiritual entity, or nobility of temperament, in this context it is one and the same).

I like to think of a writer's "voice" as the soul of their imagination. If you stay true to your soul, you will produce unique fiction. There is no doubt about it. Because everyone has his or her own soul. No other soul in this world will ever possess the exact same qualities as yours. So when you are seeking writing advice, always take into account that the advice is coming from writers with their own unique souls, too. Be inspired by them. Feel motivated. But do not feel the need to be like them. Trying to write like somebody else is (bar writing exercises), in my opinion, the biggest disservice you can do for your work.

In the first book of the *Writing in a Nutshell* Series, I focused on demonstrating how to transition "telling" into "showing." In this book, I deal with another of the most common criticisms aspiring writers face: *to absolutely avoid adverbs and clichés like the plague.* But see, right now, I just used one of each. And at the beginning of the Introduction, I used a few too. Because they come naturally, and we frequently use them in everyday speech. But in fiction, too many adverbs and clichés weaken your prose. It's considered "lazy writing," because it means we don't have to show what's happening.

If your manuscript has too many adverbs and clichés, it most likely means that the emotion you felt while writing it is not going to translate to the reader in the same way. Never underestimate the weakness of adverbs and clichés. You'd be surprised how vivid your writing will become once they are subverted.

Sure, clichés exist because they stem from things many of us experience in real life, and you may argue that they are "relatable," so why not use them? But the way in which one experiences things isn't always the same. As writers, it's your duty to make readers experience your story from a unique point of view. Your point of view.

Before we go into details about how adverbs and clichés weaken prose, and how you can subvert them, first you need to understand that they aren't always going to be a problem. In fact, you don't need to go overboard trying to eliminate every single adverb and cliché in your manuscript. Because sometimes, they just work. They serve a purpose. Especially in dialogue. Of course, it also depends a lot on your character's voice.

For example, sometimes it's more concise to write, "She knocked lightly on the door." Not every single action needs to be poetic and unique. Sometimes you need to write exactly what someone is doing because it's not important enough to draw attention to. Also, if we just wrote, "She knocked on the door," we'd have no idea whether it was loud or not. And if this action wasn't all that significant, it would be a bit too wordy to say something like, "She knocked on the door as if her hand were as light as a feather." (Look, cliché again, they creep in so easily, don't they?)

But consider this: What if this person's light knocking on the door was paramount to the story? What if it was a moment of suspense? What if behind that door was a man this person was afraid of? What if this person was anticipating being verbally abused for the interruption? Then this 'lightly knocking on the door' would have a significant purpose, yes?

The action of lightly knocking on that door is no longer a simple transitional action that moves the character from A to B. It is in your manuscript for a reason. You put it there for your readers to feel the same apprehension your character feels. And no adverb or cliché, as you can see, is going to draw attention to that moment of intensity like something crafted for it exclusively.

So let's try our hand at making this moment pop. How about, "She tapped on the door. It echoed in her ears like an axe to a carcass."

So how does this better convey its intended sentiment? I'd say the fact that this person perceives their tap on the door as a deep, echoing, and unpleasant sound means that they are anxious about the reaction it is going to elicit. Also note that I've chosen the verb (tap) which means "a light knock," so there is no reason for me to use the adverb "lightly."

So how exactly can we approach the subversion of adverbs and clichés? For starters, play around with similes and metaphors when you're trying to convey emotion, and for action, use strong verbs to show it happening in real time. For example, instead of using something clichéd like "the streets were so quiet you could hear a pin drop," find a small detail to zoom in on that shows how quiet the streets are. Put a lonely-looking man kicking rubbish down an abandoned street, perhaps. Have him drag his feet. Perhaps the sound can be heard from two blocks away where your narrator is waiting for a bus that never arrives.

Most of the time, if you think of the small details, rather than the bigger picture, you'll avoid adverbs and clichés naturally. And remember to be experimental. You never know what you might come up with.

By analyzing the thirty-four subversions of adverbs and clichés in this book, I hope you will be inspired to transform the mundane and overused expressions in your work into gourmet imagery.

I suggest you follow these steps:

Step one: For the first read-through, read each example in its entirety, to grasp the general feel of them. Notice how flat the examples using the adverbs and clichés sound compared to the unique examples.

Step two: For the second read-through, identify which elements in the unique examples match the basic sentiments of the adverbs and clichés presented in the other examples.

Step three: For the third read-through, identify how the unique example conveys, and/or adds to, those sentiments.

Step four: And for the fourth and final read-through, brainstorm your own way of subverting the examples that use the adverbs and clichés. Remember, do not try to write like me. Just be yourself. Close the book. Close your eyes. Immerse yourself in the situation.

In this print edition, I have provided some blank lined pages at the back of the book for you to jot down your notes and ideas as you read.

Three short writing prompts are also provided.

There are also separate alphabetical indexes of adverbs, and clichés.

Happy subverting!

EXAMPLE 1

Adverbs: loudly • relentlessly • slowly

Clichés: scream like a hyena • snail's pace • splitting headache • traffic jam

Using adverbs

I slowly move through the chaotic traffic, my daughter screaming loudly in the back seat. My head is throbbing relentlessly. It feels like it's going to crack open.

Using clichés

My daughter and I are stuck in a traffic jam, and it's giving me a splitting headache. The cars are moving at a snail's pace, and my daughter is screaming like a hyena.

Unique example

The sharp shrill of car horns and my daughter's wails pierce through my head like ice picks, doing nothing to help lessen my grip on the steering wheel, while we inch along in grueling traffic.

EXAMPLE 2

Adverb: habitually

Cliché: old habits die hard

Using adverb

Men are habitually stubborn.

Using cliché

Men never change. Old habits die hard.

Unique example

Men cling to habit like sap to a tree trunk.

EXAMPLE 3

Adverb: badly

Cliché: leave a bad taste in one's mouth

Using adverb

His behaviour affected me badly.

Using cliché

His behaviour left me with a bad taste in my mouth.

Unique example

The aftermath of his behaviour plagued my senses like rotten egg.

EXAMPLE 4

Adverbs: desperately • finally • freely • heavily • lightly

Clichés: as light as a feather • clean slate • feel the weight on one's shoulders • under the skin

Using adverbs

As I lightly step onto the sand, I realize I'm finally ready to start over, far from the place where I desperately feel the need to run away. I'll head to a town where regret no longer weighs heavily on me; a place where I can freely be myself.

Using clichés

I step foot onto the sand, my feet as light as feathers. I realize I'm ready for a clean slate, to start again in a new town where I no longer feel the weight of regret on my shoulders, or the strong desire to flee; a place where I'll be accepted for who I am under the skin.

Unique example

As I tiptoe out of the water, I am weightless. I'm ready to wipe this regret from my skin; to immerse myself in a new ocean, where my desire for fleeing this emotional cage hides like a mermaid ambivalent about growing legs. I'll never have to disguise my soul again.

EXAMPLE 5

Adverb: sluggishly

Cliché: dead weight

Using adverb

Her clammy hands rest sluggishly in mine.

Using cliché

Her sweaty hands rest in mine like dead weight.

Unique example

Her hands rest in mine like damp autumn leaves.

EXAMPLE 6

Adverbs: angrily • suddenly

Clichés: bristle with rage • make one's hair stand on end

Using adverbs

"How dare you," Frank says angrily. Suddenly, I feel scared.

Using clichés

Frank is bristling with so much rage that it makes my hair stand on end.

Unique example

"How dare you." Frank growls and swipes everything off my desk. The air thickens in my throat like starch in water.

EXAMPLE 7

Adverbs: always • intensely • nervously • thoroughly • truly

Clichés: break out in a cold sweat • bundle of nerves • deep down • get a kick out of • give it one's all • if you do it once, you'll do it again

Using adverbs

Stage fright is an intensely rooted fear. But despite being anxious all the time, I truly know that I thoroughly enjoy performing in front of a live audience. Once I've done it, I'll be addicted and always need another hit. And I'll no longer linger nervously at the side of the stage.

Using clichés

Despite stage fright making me break out in a cold sweat, deep down I know I get a kick out of singing for a live audience. It's like a drug: if I do it once, I want to do it again. I'm no longer a bundle of nerves, and the need to give it my all is paramount.

Unique example

Stage fright is a paralytic, a dude stiffened by tetrodotoxin. But the overall thrill of singing for a live audience survives the poison, and I wake up on the other side, ready to get back on stage. With the angst gone, the craving to perform again overpowers me like a vampire needs blood.

EXAMPLE 8

Adverbs: attentively • closely • constantly

Clichés: alarms go off in one's head • gut instinct • ignore the signs

Using adverbs

No matter how many warnings I get, I constantly ignore them. Maybe I should closely and attentively listen to my instincts.

Using clichés

I should stop ignoring the signs. Alarms keep going off in my head, but I just don't listen to my gut instincts.

Unique example

I should listen to the elusive buzz of caution, instead of flicking it away like a fly interrupting my concentration.

EXAMPLE 9

Adverb: faintly

Cliché: hear in the distance

Using adverb

The clock ticks faintly in the background.

Using cliché

I can hear the clock ticking in the distance.

Unique example

The clock ticks like a sewing needle tapping eggshell.

EXAMPLE 10

Adverbs: emotionally • morbidly • perpetually • strikingly • stylishly • woefully

Clichés: down in the mouth • dressed to kill • keep at bay • ooh and ahh • put pressure on oneself • sense of self-pride

Using adverbs

I stare at myself, dressed stylishly in black, in the TV screen. There's something morbidly beautiful and dark about my reflection and how it woefully matches the ambivalence I feel about myself right now. Wouldn't it be great if I could perpetually stay in there? I'd be praised by others all day long for my strikingly stunning pose, and abolish my judgmental inner-voice. I might feel emotionally stable again.

Using clichés

I stare at my reflection in the TV screen. Though I may be dressed to kill, I sure don't feel that way. I feel down in the mouth and insecure about myself, but I feel a small sense of self pride too. I wish I was a painting on a wall. Onlookers would ooh and ahh at my striking gothic beauty, and I'd stop putting so much pressure on myself to please others. I might keep my emotional instability at bay.

Unique example

The TV is off. I stare at my reflection in the screen. I'm an eighteenth-century portrait on canvas, in a grey hue, as if painted in darkness. Much like the darkness I live inside my head. If only I could remain in that reflection—motionless, flushed with gothic candor, a drifter in a place where I will never judge myself; a place where I can be hung in a gallery and praised rather than scrutinized for my unconventional individuality.

EXAMPLE 11

Adverbs: practically • remarkably • smoothly • sweetly

Clichés: eye candy • so (adj) one could eat it

Using adverbs

Mike is remarkably handsome, and he speaks so smoothly and sweetly in his British accent, I can practically taste it.

Using clichés

Mike is pure eye candy, and his British accent is so smooth and sweet I could just eat it.

Unique example

Mike's picture should be on the front page of Who. And you should hear him speak. His British accent is like crème caramel.

EXAMPLE 12

Adverb: rhythmically

Cliché: to the beat of one's heart

Using adverb

Eli rhythmically flicks a teaspoon in his palm.

Using cliché

Eli flicks a teaspoon in his palm to the beat of my heart.

Unique example

Eli flicks a teaspoon in his palm. It thumps like a weak heart in a distant stethoscope.

EXAMPLE 13

Adverbs: coolly • creatively • extremely • genuinely • positively • utterly

Clichés: elixir of life • flight of fancy • have a gift • in one's blood • it's not a crime • one can dream • pause in thought • unvarnished truth • vivid imagination

Using adverbs

"My presence is so positively calming, your daughter wishes she could drink it." Dr. Morris smiled coolly. "Of course, that is an utterly unrealistic yearning, but she likes to creatively express herself. And I do not believe this to be a threat to her psychological well-being. I believe observations such as these are extremely intelligent." Dr. Morris seemed genuinely pleased with my daughter's progress, but I wasn't convinced.

Using clichés

"My presence makes your daughter feel so calm, she claims it could be her elixir of life." Dr. Morris had no qualms about telling us the unvarnished truth of our daughter's psychological health. "Of course, this is merely a flight of fancy, but one can dream, yes? Regardless, having such a vivid imagination is in her blood. It's not a crime." Dr. Morris pauses in thought. "In fact, I believe she may have a gift."

Unique example

"My companionship seems to instill a sense of calm in your daughter. I quote: 'I wish I could catch your presence in a jar, leave it on my mantle, and take self-prescribed sips from it when needed.' Extraordinary, yes?" Dr. Morris nodded, as if trying to convince himself that her remark was worthy of admiration. "It may seem idealistic, but everybody's minds do indeed adjust one's reality to fulfill one's emotional needs." He smiles, squints at a painting on his wall. "I don't believe there is anything wrong with being so imaginative. No. No, not at all."

EXAMPLE 14

> **Adverbs:** furiously • totally

> **Clichés:** behave like (n) is invisible • blow a gasket

Using adverbs

My colleagues totally ignore me. It makes me furiously mad.

Using clichés

My colleagues get on with their work as if I'm invisible. I think I'm going to blow a gasket.

Unique example

My colleagues' persistent disregard for my presence pisses me off like an un-locatable itch.

EXAMPLE 15

Adverb: tremendously

Cliché: I could eat a horse

Using adverb

I'm tremendously hungry.

Using cliché

I'm so hungry I could eat a horse.

Unique example

If you put me in an eating contest, I'd win. Not only would I win, I'd go out for dinner afterward to celebrate!

EXAMPLE 16

Adverbs: eventually • merrily • recklessly

Clichés: as happy as Larry (AmE: a clam) • as tough as nails • before you know it • black and blue • do (n) like there's no tomorrow • go hell for leather

Using adverbs

My three-year-old son is sitting merrily on my shoulders at the party. He thinks I'm as strong as daddy and recklessly swings his arms and legs around to the music, kicking and punching me everywhere, oblivious to the damage he's doing. Eventually, my chest is covered in ghastly bruises.

Using clichés

My three-year-old son is as happy as Larry sitting on my shoulders at the party. He thinks I'm as tough as nails, just like daddy, and goes hell for leather, swinging his arms and legs around to the music like there's no tomorrow. Before I know it, my chest is black and blue.

Unique example

My three-year-old son and I are at the party. I feel vibrations in my shoulders as he giggles to the music. But sometimes I think he forgets who he's sitting on and swings his limbs around like a rag doll in a washing machine. Before long, bruises stain my chest like a white blouse washed with black socks.

EXAMPLE 17

Adverb: mournfully

Cliché: bawl one's eyes out

Using adverb

I'm weeping mournfully.

Using cliché

I'm so sad that I bawl my eyes out.

Unique example

My tears erupt like storm water from a cracked drain pipe.

EXAMPLE 18

Adverb: tragically

Cliché: pour one's heart out

Using adverb

The clarinet sounds tragically sad in this song.

Using cliché

The clarinet in this song sounds like it's pouring its heart out.

Unique example

In this song, the clarinet is a wilting willow, pleading to be left in solitude to wither and fade.

EXAMPLE 19

Adverbs: frankly • persistently • somewhat • successfully

Clichés: achieve one's goals • clutching at (AmE: grasping for) straws • no pain, no gain • reach for the stars • run into obstacles • see the light at the end of the tunnel • so be it

Using adverbs

I've persistently been doing everything and anything I can to reach my goals successfully. Yeah, my goals are somewhat impossible to achieve, but so what? I like the challenge. Frankly, I only have one wish. If I can't get what I want without a struggle, then please give me an obstacle that I can at least overcome. I can't cope with moving backward all the time.

Using clichés

All these years, I've been clutching at straws to achieve my goals. Sure, I've been reaching for the stars, and they're a long way away. But no pain, no gain, right? If I can't get what I want without running into anymore obstacles, then so be it. But give me one that I can overcome, so that I can at least see the light at the end of the tunnel.

Unique example

All these years, I've been trying to cross an ocean via a never-ending bridge made of fraying string. My goals may seem unrealistic to some. Though I walk backward sometimes, I haven't slipped off the bridge. Yet. All I long for is the day when my only obstacle is a narrow creek I can drop a plank of wood over. I can even fall in if you like. I don't care if I get all muddy. As long as I make it across.

EXAMPLE 20

Adverbs: completely • sleepily

Clichés: close, but no cigar • dog-tired

Using adverbs

I sleepily reach for my mobile phone, but my coordination is completely off and I grab my hair brush instead.

Using clichés

Still dog-tired, I reach for my mobile phone on the bedside table. Close, but no cigar.

Unique example

I reach for the mobile phone on my bedside table as if my hand were a sea lion flipper.

EXAMPLE 21

Adverb: rapidly

Cliché: racing heart

Using adverb

My heart beats rapidly.

Using cliché

My heart races.

Unique example

My heart beats like a cog train gaining speed.

EXAMPLE 22

Adverbs: barely • definitely • hardly • painfully • really • very • violently

Clichés: in way over one's head • off the charts • speck of dust • the best of one's ability • time flies

Using adverbs

It doesn't seem very long ago since giving birth to Valerie. It's barely been a year. In hospital, I remember thinking that I'd definitely need drugs. But I wasn't really thinking straight and lost the opportunity. While giving birth, I was painfully aware of every spasm in my body. I can hardly believe that what was once so tiny became so big, and pushed through me so violently.

Using clichés

Time has flown by since giving birth to Valerie. I remember thinking that I'd gotten myself in way over my head. I'd put off asking for an epidural to the best of my ability, but then when I decided I needed it, it was too late. I can't believe Valerie was once as small as a speck of dust, and grew so big, and then pushed through such a small opening. The pain, let me tell you, was off the charts.

Unique example

I gave birth to Valerie a year ago. That year has gone by so fast I often wonder if I still have toes. I can still feel my legs in those stirrups—the sweaty doctor sucking the entire universe through my spasming black hole, too late to ask for chemical courage. Muscles pulled from my spine, my thighs to my pelvis, every push a deliberate infliction of pain. What began as an insignificant seed, thrust itself through me like a fist tearing through fabric.

EXAMPLE 23

Adverb: deadly

Cliché: never felt so (adj) in one's life

Using adverb

I'm deadly relaxed.

Using cliché

I have never felt so relaxed in my life. I feel like I'm going to lose consciousness!

Unique example

My body sinks into the sofa like a hollow log in quicksand.

EXAMPLE 24

Adverbs: defiantly • slightly

Clichés: find the key to one's heart • the lights are on but nobody's home • windows of one's soul

Using adverbs

I lean forward slightly, looking defiantly into his eyes. But they seem full of so much nothingness. I guess he just doesn't want to let me in.

Using clichés

I lean forward, close enough to peer into the windows of his soul. The lights are on, but there doesn't seem to be anyone home. I guess I'll never find the key to his heart.

Unique example

I lean forward. But I can't see past my fishbowl reflection in his eyes' watery sheen. They're like double-glazed windows. You can see through them, but you can't hear what's happening on the other side.

EXAMPLE 25

> **Adverb:** simultaneously

> **Cliché:** all at once

Using adverb

All five people speak simultaneously.

Using cliché

The five people speak all at once.

Unique example

Their five voices overlap like a tuning orchestra.

EXAMPLE 26

Adverb: offensively

Cliché: dust bunnies

Using adverb

My bed sheets are offensively dusty.

Using cliché

My bed sheets are full of dust bunnies.

Unique example

Getting into bed is like stepping into a vacuum cleaner bag.

EXAMPLE 27

Adverbs: basically • eternally • highly • mainly
• mightily

Clichés: call the shots • different shapes and
sizes • do as one pleases • leave one's
mark on (n)

Using adverbs

He mainly wants to become influential, and to
be eternally free to follow as many different
paths as he desires, to basically see, and do, the
undiscovered, to become highly respected and call
out mightily to the world: "I am your President!"

Using clichés

He wants to leave his mark on the world; to forever
be free to do as he pleases, to follow paths of
all different shapes and sizes; to make the world's
population gloat over him, and know that he is the
only one who calls the shots.

Unique example

He wants to make some noise; enough to bulldoze a permanent exit from this dead-end life, giving access to a new and undiscovered highway; to hear the influence of his motivation, his determination, echo through a football stadium like a thousand bass drums beating the thunderous rhythm of world domination.

EXAMPLE 28

> **Adverb:** unusually

> **Cliché:** hard as rock

Using adverb

Donna's hairdo looks unusually stiff.

Using cliché

Donna's hairdo looks as hard as rock.

Unique example

Donna's hairdo looks as if it's been sprayed in position since 1982.

EXAMPLE 29

Adverb: madly

Cliché: like bees to honey

Using adverb

Women are madly attracted to Frank.

Using cliché

Frank attracts women like bees to honey.

Unique example

What an atheist is to a Jehovah's Witness, Frank is to women.

EXAMPLE 30

Adverbs: antagonistically • boldly

Clichés: crumble under pressure • smile like a Cheshire Cat • stare someone down

Using adverbs

Adam smiles, and antagonistically stares at me. But I boldly refuse to succumb to his manipulation.

Using clichés

Adam smiles like a Cheshire Cat and tries to stare me down. But I will not crumble under the pressure.

Unique example

With an arrogant grin, Adam glares at me. He may be fire. But I am not ice.

EXAMPLE 31

Adverbs: eagerly • erratically • proudly

Clichés: have ants in one's pants • pride and joy
• scan every inch

Using adverbs

Her eyes move erratically, left to right, eagerly searching for the perfect position on the wall to proudly hang her new piece of art.

Using clichés

She scans every inch of our four walls like she's got ants in her pants, trying to locate a spot to hang her art. It's her new pride and joy.

Unique example

Her eyes dart from wall to wall, as if hunting down a mosquito, trying to determine the perfect position to display her very first "masterpiece."

EXAMPLE 32

Adverb: tenderly

Cliché: tingling up and down one's spine

Using adverb

He tenderly stroked my cheek and it made my skin feel all tingly.

Using cliché

When he stroked my cheek I felt tingling up and down my spine.

Unique example

When he stroked my cheek, it tingled as if he was transferring energy into my soul.

EXAMPLE 33

Adverb: swiftly

Cliché: in one fell swoop

Using adverb

Eva swiftly grabs her thesis from the drawer.

Using cliché

In one fell swoop, Eva snatches her thesis from the drawer.

Unique example

Eva scoops her thesis from the drawer like an eagle catching prey.

EXAMPLE 34

Adverbs: consciously • consistently • fondly • idly • merely • never • reluctantly • soon

Clichés: collect dust • come to terms with • have a mind of one's own • only a matter of time • stay in shape • toy with an idea • withstand the test of time

Using adverbs

I used to think fondly of my second-hand acoustic guitar and how she consistently stayed in tune. I pretended she was consciously aware of her existence, and determined to never give up. When I reluctantly sold her, I felt better knowing she wouldn't sit idly in a shop window. She would soon convince another person to play her again by merely tempting them with her beauty.

Using clichés

I used to love my second-hand acoustic guitar for how she withstood the test of time. I liked to toy with the idea that she had a mind of her own, and that's how she stayed in such good shape. When I sold her, it helped me come to terms with letting her go, knowing she wouldn't sit in a corner collecting dust; knowing it would only be a matter of time before her unique splendor tempted somebody to play her again.

Unique example

I used to admire my second-hand acoustic guitar as if she were a rare antique chair, contemplating her own remarkable existence, reminiscing about all the generations of people who had used her before me. When I sold her, it was comforting to think that no matter how many times people walked past her in the display window, she understood that everyone appreciated her beauty, her universal function. That one day, someone would purchase her, cherish her, and play her with love.

NOW IT'S YOUR TURN

Change the following into something unique without the use of adverbs or clichés:

1. I wake up. My lips slowly become unstuck as I yawn. I have a feeling that something is terribly wrong. I quickly sit upright in bed and gaze out the window. It's raining cats and dogs.

2. Lila swiftly packed up her belongings and fled the hotel in the blink of an eye. There was no way she was going to let herself get caught now. Not after travelling through hell and high water to finally find these diamonds.

3. I was so surprised at his announcement that my jaw dropped! My friend must have been so embarrassed by my behaviour because she had to physically close my mouth for me. How dare he do this? Who does he think he is to drop such a bombshell?

BOOK #3

The Six Senses in a Nutshell
Demonstrated Transitions from Bleak to Bold Narrative

BOOK #3 CONTENTS

INTRODUCTION

In the first two books in this series, I demonstrated the distinct difference between "telling" and "showing," and how you can turn those dreaded adverbs and clichés into exciting and unique imagery.

If you've read Books 1 and 2 of the *Writing in a Nutshell* series, you'll know that my own writing struggles led me to write these pocket-sized writing guides—so you can learn to hone your craft in bite-sized, manageable pieces. But let me reiterate something I said in Books 1 and 2, because I think it's very important to stress this: the purpose of this series is to inspire you to become better at your craft. To teach you how to grow as a writer. It will not tell you how to write. It will not preach writing rules and styles to you. But it will help you to realize that you can, little by little, end up with a brilliant piece of work.

I hope that this book—and if you've read all three, this series—inspires and motivates you to become a better writer. But please do not feel like you need to write like me. Everyone has their own style. Trying to write like somebody else is (bar writing exercises), in my opinion, the biggest disservice you can do for your work. So just remember: be yourself.

In this book, *The Six Senses in a Nutshell*, I show you

how utilizing the six senses (*see*, *hear*, *smell*, *taste*, *touch*, and *instinct*) can really bring your writing to life. To do this successfully, you need to "show, not tell". Otherwise, these senses will not really be senses. The reader won't actually experience them, they will only "read about" them. And the whole point of reading a great book is to feel like you aren't actually reading. Right? Right. Using the six senses in an effective way will accomplish this.

The key to using sense in your writing, however, is to limit your use of the words, *see*, *feel*, *hear*, *smell* and *taste*. That's not to say you shouldn't ever use these words, but just be aware you don't overuse them.

The most ideal way to incorporate senses is to employ language in which sense is already a part of. For example, instead of saying the kitchen smelled sweet with melted chocolate, show the reader what's cooking, and consequently that taste and scent will be present in the narrative without you having to point it out.

Using the six senses well is also not only about having your characters sense things, it's about making your readers sense things—even elements that your characters aren't feeling, i.e., if the reader knows more than your character(s) do, or if you're showing something that you might react to differently than the characters in the book. You'll better understand what I mean when you read the eleven* transitions in this book.

In each demonstrated transition I provide a BLEAK passage (prose lacking sensory information), and a BOLD passage (the BLEAK passage revamped to make it more appealing by utilizing sense in an indirect and/or stimulating way).

So, how should you use this book?

Step one: Read through the BLEAK passage. Make notes on what senses it is lacking, or what senses could be added. Then, isolate each sentence. How would you revamp it to give it more life? (Your rewrite can extend beyond one sentence and include things that are not already present to make the scene more stimulating.) Before reading my BOLD passage, I want you to write your own. I've always believed a writer learns better by "doing," and then correcting the mistakes. That way you become more aware of the level of improvement you're making, and how you're making it.

Step two: Put your BOLD attempt aside and read my BOLD passage. As you're reading, see if you can match the sentences you isolated in the BLEAK passage to any of the content in my BOLD passage. Briefly consider how the content has changed, developed, and acquired more life, but do not start analyzing it yet.

Step three: Read through the WHICH SENSES

HAVE BEEN USED AND HOW? section. I provide you with my own break down of the first sentence(s) of my BOLD passage, and tell you what senses have been used, and what/how they might make the reader feel. Remember, this is my interpretation of the content. We all know that every reader interprets what they read differently due to the influence of their own experiences. The key is to make people sense something, even if what they sense ends up being different to someone else. So don't feel let down if my interpretation is different to yours—you didn't do anything wrong. We are all unique individuals. Also note that when I use the word "feel" as a sense, I'm referring to both the physical (touch) and intuitive (sixth sense).

Step four: Now mimic what I've done in the WHICH SENSES HAVE BEEN USED AND HOW? section, for the rest of my BOLD passage. Isolate each sentence of the text and write down which senses it utilizes and how.

Please note, however, that some sentences within a passage will not be overflowing with sensory information. Sometimes we need to break it up with simple transitional language to avoid sensory overload. This is why the examples in this book are lengthier than in *Show & Tell in a Nutshell*. I wanted to provide you with meatier text, but at the same time, not go too over the top.

Mind you, there also might be some passages

that you feel are rife with what some people call "purple prose," i.e flowery language (Transition #1 for example). So, I just want to make sure you're aware that this is my literary/poetic style, and even though some people do not necessarily enjoy this style of writing, I think it's perfect for illustrating the point I'm making with this book.

Step five: Look at your own attempt at the BLEAK passage. Now improve it.

Step six: After you've been through the eleven transitions, look at the NOW WHAT? section at the end of the book, where there is an additional writing exercise.

Note: You'll notice that this book doesn't have an Index of Senses. That's because if I included one, it would give away all the answers and contaminate your own interpretation of the texts. I've suggested, in the NOW WHAT? section, that you create your own for future reference. There is space at the back of the book to do so where I have provided some lined note-taking pages.

By following these steps, I hope you will be inspired to transform the bleak into bold. Remember, just be yourself. And please don't feel ashamed to write in this book. It's what it's made for.

Happy writing!

Why 11 transitions, and not an even 10 or 12? Because in numerology, it is a Master Number and represents intuition, which is the sixth sense. Fitting, yes?

TRANSITION 1

Bleak

The island is very beautiful, extremely hot, and all the houses are white with colourful wooden windows. In the mornings, it can get very noisy too, especially with all the insects and animals left free to roam wherever they like. And the bread truck makes a decent amount of racket. But it's so wonderful how people get their bread delivered. Beats going to the supermarket, that's for sure. I think the people that live there are a bit weird though—they give me the creeps for some reason. But I do love living on this island because it's very relaxing. And when the heat gets too much to handle, all you have to do is jump into the sea to cool off. It's absolute bliss!

Bold

The island's windy mountainous roads are framed with olive groves and air so crisp you could snap it like celery. The houses are stained with whitewash and embedded with old-style wooden shutters, tailored by the locals to keep the summer swelter out. They are painted blue, red, or green, but occasionally you may come across the odd pink or orange shutters, which are more often than not inhabited by the eccentric barmy type who are colour-blind, or the young and loaded foreigner who believes an island revolution should be in order.

Goats meander about the streets, butting each other's heads senselessly as they try to escape oncoming cars and motorcycles. The roosters, chickens, and geese fire up the locals at the first sign of sunrise. Birds chirp, cicadas "jijiga" in the olive trees, and dogs bark as the bread truck, a red beat-up Ute, delivers fresh hot loaves to each residence, and slips the required amount of bread into handmade cloth bags hanging from wire fencing.

Summer on this island engraves your skin with a longing to spend sunrise to sunset lying on a small, empty, white-pebbled beach in a secluded cove at the end of a private dirt track. At midday, it gets so hot you need to wade through the heat waves rising from the uneven tarred road like kindred spirits before you can wade in the Ionian Sea to cool off—a flat, motionless oil bath which glows with an infinite turquoise glint. It may seem you are stepping into velvet, however, you emerge covered in a thin salty crust you can brush off like sand when it dries.

WHICH SENSES HAVE BEEN USED AND HOW?

Let me get you started ...

E.g., "The island's windy mountainous roads are framed with olive groves and air so crisp you could snap it like celery."

see • feel • smell • taste

What can you see?
Vast green, olive trees, windy roads, steep hills

What can you feel?
A fresh breeze brush against my skin. It's not actually written, but it's there between the lines.

What can you smell or taste?
Fresh crisp celery, which denotes the feeling of fresh air, and perhaps a little condensation

Read the BOLD example again. Isolate each sentence and identify what senses are being utilized, and how.

TRANSITION 2

Bleak

The sun shone through the window. The living room was dusty and the furniture was in the same place it had always been for the previous twenty-five years. The interior design was ancient, and looked as depressed as the people who lived there, including Fran.

Fran watched TV commercials with the volume down—everyone and everything looked fake and overcompensated. It almost made her feel ashamed to be Australian.

The crickets were making a lot of noise. So were all the appliances in the kitchen.

Everything was so loud.

And so monotonous.

Fran had to get out of here.

Bold

The sun bled an orange glucose shard of light through the dusty blinds. Thick dust layered the TV screen, no longer camouflaged by the night. For Fran's entire life, the TV had sat in this exact position. In the corner. On a mahogany treasure chest with an intricately designed rusty metal latch. Not once in her twenty-five years had the furniture been moved around. She couldn't even remember the rug under the coffee table being removed, or steam-cleaned. But somehow everything had remained tidy, soulless, covered by an invisible sheen of emotional filth. A happy homemaker's cocoon inhabited by the manically depressed who succeeded in making others believe they were perfectly fine. Fran was not an exception.

Fran watched commercials in mute—graceful images of happy blonde, blue-eyed nuclear families eating Vegemite sandwiches in abnormally green and large grassy backyards. Images of zealous teens throwing Frisbees and rubber balls for Golden Retrievers that didn't need to be given orders, and of dogs herding sheep like obedient robots. Of young, outrageously cute crystal-eyed siblings hugging and kissing each other, as if they'd never thrown tantrums over toy-snatching. Of parents looking impossibly content, barbequing up a feast for their statistically calculated 2.5 kids, under an fake cloudless sky. All in all, a stereotypical view of Australia, distorted by blank sound, with raging lawn mowers as backdrop.

The crickets had just begun their nightly symphonic orchestra. The fridge shuddered. The water filter bubbled. The clock ticked. The kitchen tap dripped … waste-ing-wor-tah.

I'm going to go mad if I don't leave, Fran thought.

WHICH SENSES HAVE BEEN USED AND HOW?

Let me get you started …

E.g., "The sun bled an orange glucose shard of light through the dusty blinds."

> see • feel • smell

What can you see?
Dim orange sun light, dust in the air, window with blinds slightly open

What can you feel?
Warm, yet stuffy and downbeat, perhaps a tickly nose from the dust

What can you smell?
A musty room, yet slightly sweet; the impression that the air is thick and oppressive

Read the BOLD example again. Isolate each sentence and identify what senses are being utilized, and how.

TRANSITION 3

Bleak

Nelly feels so drunk and dizzy from all the visual and aural stimulation in this night club that she thinks she might soon throw up.

"Darling, I think we'd better get you home," Hans says, helping her up. "Can you walk?"

"Um ... yep." Nelly stands, and pretends to be fine. She'll be glad to get a breath of air after being so long in that stuffy club.

Out on the street, the cold air somewhat revitalizes her senses. When her cell vibrates in her handbag, Hans makes a sarcastic remark about her shock. Nelly sighs at the ridiculous hour she's receiving a call and almost loses balance searching her bag for the phone.

"Hello?"

"Oh good, I haven't woken you up. I had a feeling you'd be out and about."

"What do you want?"

"I might be close to finding Dan."

Dan? What?

"But I don't want to see Dan. I hate the bastard. You know that! Why would you even bother, Carol?"

Nelly and Carol end up arguing and hanging up on bad terms. But Nelly suddenly feels awful about the way she spoke to her and is afraid she may have lost her only true friend.

Bold

Nelly looks up at Hans's wavering foggy face and the tri-image of the large TV screen of the Pet Shop Boys' Absolutely Fabulous video clip pounding on the large screen overhead. Her body convulses forward and she cups a hand to her mouth, stunting the vomit in its tracks.

"Darling, I think we'd better get you home."

Nelly nods, managing to keep the spew at bay. Hans grabs Nelly's bag and helps her to stand. "Can you walk?"

"Um … yep." She stands, holds her head high, straightens her silver spandex boob tube above her breasts, and fakes it. At least until they get out of the claustrophobic, and overly smoke-machined atmosphere where she can take a nice deep breath.

Out on the street, waiting for a cab, the sharp early morning air cuts right through her, bringing her senses back to life and turning her entertaining drunken dizziness and drugged bounce into a sick whirlpool of indignation. The sound of cars on wet roads whoosh through her ears as if she's listening to panned sound effects through headphones. She clutches her handbag under her arm when the ground starts to pulsate. She looks at Hans as if something is sawing her in half.

"Honey," Hans says, lighting a cigarette, "death isn't embedded into your side. It's your cell. Vibrating."

Nelly loosens her grip and sighs in relief. She searches her bag for the phone.

"What the hell time is it? 4:00 a.m.?" Nelly rolls her eyes at Hans. He chuckles when she almost loses balance and starts to walk backward. She grabs the phone, stops in the middle of the sidewalk holding one arm out to her side as if ready to launch into flight.

"Hello?"

"Oh good, I haven't woken you. I had a feeling you'd be out and about."

"Carol. Why are you calling me so late?"

"What's wrong? You're awake, aren't you?"

"What do you want?"

"I might be close to finding Dan."

Nelly pulls the phone away from her ear and glares at the keypad as if it has a voice of its own. She looks at Hans who shrugs in question. She puts the phone back to her ear.

"What the hell?"

"Yeah, I know. After all these years. Come home. Let's try and meet up with him together?"

"Don't be ridiculous, Carol. Why on earth would I want to do that for? I'm finally getting my shit together."

"I'm discovering some serious stuff, Nelly, and I think you should be here. I think we should do this together."

Nelly coughs in disgust as if Carol's request has regurgitated bile.

"Carol, I don't know what kind of world you're living in, but it's not mine. Okay? I don't give a damn about Dan or about any of the 'serious shit' you're finding out. Let me live my life, and you live yours. Maybe you can try to do that on your own for once too, huh? Or would you like me to hire someone to hold your hand now that I'm not around anymore?"

Nelly cringes at Carol's quick inward breath as if trying to ignore the hurt.

"But don't you want to know what happened to him?"

Nelly closes her eyes. Remembers the time he left

her for dead in a ditch ...

"I don't care. Plus, I've already caught up with him and told him to never contact me again."

"You what?"

Silence thickens in Nelly's ear.

"How could you not ..."

"Say anything? Oh, I don't know. Maybe because some people don't talk about things simply because they don't want crap in their lives. Maybe because my life is mine, and I can do what I like with it? Got it?"

"But, I thought we ... loved each other," Carol gurgles. "I thought we were a team. I thought we agreed to seek revenge. Together."

"Grow up, Carol. Things change."

Carol sobs. A pinch of pain expands in Nelly's stomach like a chemical contamination, swelling, gushing through her mouth in torrents. "Stop calling me. Learn to live without me. Our whole family should be fed to the wolves."

Nelly hangs up the phone and throws it in her bag. She lifts her head, her mind and body flooded with freedom and guilty triumph, to see Hans's hand cupped over his mouth, and tears streaming down his cheeks. At this moment, she realizes, she has just pushed away the only person in the world she unconditionally loves. And that she may never be able to get her back.

WHICH SENSES HAVE BEEN USED AND HOW?

Let me get you started ...

E.g., "Nelly looks up at Hans's wavering foggy face and the tri-image of the large TV screen of the Pet Shop Boys' Absolutely Fabulous video clip pounding on the large screen overhead. Her body convulses forward and she cups a hand to her mouth, stunting a vomit warning in its tracks."

---

see • feel • taste • hear

What can you see?
A blurry vision of a person's face and video clip

What can you feel?
Dizziness, nausea

What can you taste?
Alcohol, vomit

What can you hear?
Loud music

Read the BOLD example again. Isolate each sentence and identify what senses are being utilized, and how.

TRANSITION 4

Bleak

As soon as Samantha arrived home a gusty wind started up. She looked at the small garden she'd attempted to landscape the previous year and was reminded of how she had failed to keep it alive. Except for one stubborn lemon tree. She felt like such a disappointment that even the brass lion-head knocker on her front door seemed to mock her.

She didn't want to go inside. Especially since he was home. She could hear him playing computer games. The sound of cars, and his frustration, came wafting out the open window. Suddenly he switched off the game.

Samantha quietly stepped inside and left her briefcase by the door hoping her son might get nosey, take a peek inside, and find her journal.

She felt uneasy, but tried not to let it show as she headed to the kitchen where her son seemed to be scouring for food in the fridge. And behaving like a pig. As usual.

"What's up, Mark?"

Mark made a rude gesture and walked out without

uttering a word.

"Don't you just walk away from me," Samantha yelled. "You come back and apologize."

Samantha sat at the kitchen table and looked around. The place was a pigsty and smelled like someone had thrown up their dessert.

As Mark locked himself in his room and turned his music on at full volume, she realized how trapped she felt in her own home.

Bold

The wind blew Samantha's blouse flat against her back as she scanned the overgrown section of grass where she'd attempted to landscape a mini rock garden last year. The pile of decorative pebbles were now lost in weeds, and fermenting apricots. The tiny lemon tree even struggled to survive on its own, producing one lemon a year, as if too stubborn to be conquered by human neglect.

Samantha stood on her doorstep, briefcase in hand, staring at the brass lion-head knocker. Every time she returned home, she was sure she could hear the lion spitting at her: *You never learn, do you woman?*

She didn't want to go inside. She never wanted to go inside. He'd be waiting for her, ready to pounce, either with degrading comments or silence; she didn't know which one was worse. But she's got to stop doing this. Working late every night wouldn't fix the relationship between them. It wouldn't fix him.

As she inserted her key, the sound of a car screeching and crashing leaped from the open living room window. He'd left the fly-wire off. Again.

Something fell to the floor and thick thuds followed—a bit of bookcase abuse, perhaps. The roar of the digital explosion stopped abruptly. Perhaps he'd turned off the TV.

She opened the door slow enough for the hinges not to squeak and stepped inside, placed her briefcase delicately by the door as she did every night—easy access for the following morning. No. The real reason was because she hoped her son would open it and read the journal she left in there. The one that's all about her struggles coping with him. Maybe he'd feel sorry for her and realize how manipulative he was.

Samantha took a deep breath, adjusted the cuffs and collar of her blouse, pushed her hair behind her ears and rubbed her chapped lips together.

She strode down the hallway, head high, toward the kitchen at the other end. Her son's shadow rippled over the tiled floor as she approached the arched entrance way. The fridge door opened and closed. Its contents rattled like the music of water-filled crystal glasses. Along with a running bath, it was perhaps the only other relaxing sound she ever heard in this household.

Her son scoffed, snorted, coughed, spat into the sink. Samantha could hear it splatter like fresh fish gut. She leaned against the archway, folded her arms under her breasts, and tried to drill a hole through his head with her glare.

"What's up, Mark?" Samantha raised her eyebrows, trying to maintain assertion.

Mark looked up and smirked, shoved a hand down the front of his jeans and rearranged his package. Samantha scanned him up and down in disgust. Mark winked, spat into the sink again, and walked out without uttering a word.

"Don't you just walk away from me," Samantha called toward the ceiling, trying to disguise her tears with volume. "You come back and apologize."

Samantha pulled out a chair and sat at the kitchen table. The counter and sink overflowed with dirty dishes. And there was something pink and sticky, cough syrup perhaps, all over the floor by the dishwasher, and brown broken glass at the base of the garbage bin.

Samantha jumped in her seat as Mark's bedroom door slammed and the boom of heavy metal sucked the oxygen right out of the air.

This was a prison.

And she'd built it herself.

WHICH SENSES HAVE BEEN USED AND HOW?

Let me get you started ...

E.g., "The wind blows Samantha's blouse flat against her back as she looks at the round overgrown patch of grass where she attempted to landscape a mini rock garden last year."

> see • feel • hear • smell

What can you see?
Samantha's garden that leaves a lot to be desired

What can you feel?
Strong wind, the silky material of a blouse brush against skin

What can you hear?
Wind, leaves rustling

What can you smell?
Grass, perhaps dead flowers/plants/weeds.

Read the BOLD example again. Isolate each sentence and identify what senses are being utilized, and how.

TRANSITION 5

Bleak

While Gary lies on his back on the grass by the river the noises of the city surround him.

He closes his eyes, flicks his cigarette in the river, and tries not to feel guilty about polluting the earth. What difference is one cigarette going to make anyway?

He screams his testament to the sky and finally—finally—he cries and releases his stress.

Bold

Gary doesn't move from his position on the grass by the river—flat on his back. He closes his eyes. Cyclists' chains clink as they glide by his head; cars rumble on the bridge behind him; leaves rustle in the wind. The sun disappears. Thunder cracks. Rain pelts down.

He flicks his cigarette toward the river knowing it won't even make it close. This time he doesn't feel guilty. The river is brown. City brown shit pollution crap, what-the-hell-are-we-doing-wrong brown.

What's one more fag?

What's one more sorry broken soul taking his stress out on the river?

What difference does it make?

"What difference does it bloody make?" he roars, punching both fists and feet repeatedly toward the sky.

And then it finally happens with one huge breath of wet air.

He cries.

He cries, and his body trembles against the earth.

WHICH SENSES HAVE BEEN USED AND HOW?

Let me get you started ...

E.g., "Gary doesn't move from his position on the grass by the river—flat on his back. He closes his eyes. Cyclists' chains clink as they glide by his head; cars rumble on the bridge behind him; leaves rustle in the wind."

---

see • feel • hear • smell

What can you see?
The sky, and then pitch black

What can you feel?
Grass, wind

What can you hear?
The river, bicycles, and cars in motion, rustling leaves

What can you smell?
City smog, grass, perhaps the river if you envision one that is polluted

Read the BOLD example again. Isolate each sentence and identify what senses are being utilized, and how.

TRANSITION 6

Bleak

Joe sits down for his morning coffee, tobacco and papers in front of the TV, and wishes his daughter Sandra would just go on a diet already.

He goes through the motions of pinching the tobacco and rolling the paper as he waits for Sandra to finish in the kitchen. He holds it up to the light and admires his handiwork.

Sandra finally comes and sits down next to him and takes the cigarette out of Joe's fingers. Joe watches her light it, and smoke it all in almost one breath.

Joe looks at Sandra with pity and hopes that she listens to his advice before it's too late. He'll always love her no matter what she looks like. But he also wants her to love herself.

Bold

Joe switches the channel one last time, leans over the coffee table, sips his double espresso, and gathers his packet of Drum, filters, papers, to roll a few cigs. He can sense Sandra's laser-like stare from behind the kitchen counter as he lodges the first rollie behind his right ear. She's urging him to let her off the hook. But he won't give in again. For the sake of her health, if anything. What kind of father would he be if he didn't put his foot down once in a while?

"Another week. And you won't feel so hungry."

Joe listens to the steadiness of his breath, watches as his calloused and bitten fingertips pinch tobacco into a neat line across the paper as though a different brain were giving his hands the orders. He rolls the tobacco between his thumbs and forefingers, licks the edge of the paper, seals it into a perfect silky cylinder. Without looking up from the coffee table, he holds the cigarette in the air.

Sandra drags her heavy feet across the carpet. A sound Joe associates with the Rottweiler they had when his ex-wife was still around.

Sandra snatches the cigarette and sits next to Joe. The leather couch sinks with a sigh. He turns to her, head still hanging, tilted to the side. She lights the cigarette with a match from her black polo shirt pocket. With only one drag, half of it disappears. Joe scrutinizes Sandra's puffy cheeks and baby-like fat that's starting to form a double chin. He still thinks she's cute. But if she keeps going like this he's worried he'll start to find his own daughter ugly. His throat tightens and he squints at her before kissing her forehead.

WHICH SENSES HAVE BEEN USED AND HOW?

Let me get you started ...

E.g., "Joe switches the channel one last time, leans over the coffee table, sips his double espresso, and gathers his packet of Drum, filters, papers, to roll a few cigs."

> see • feel • taste • hear • smell

What can you see?
TV, coffee table, coffee, cigarette papers, tobacco

What can you feel?
Cigarette/papers/filter packets, handle of the espresso cup; perhaps boredom and/or morning blues?

What can you taste?
Coffee, tobacco

What can you hear?
Voices from the TV

What can you smell?
Coffee, tobacco

Read the BOLD example again. Isolate each sentence and identify what senses are being utilized, and how.

TRANSITION 7

Bleak

I've just come home from the beach. I stand outside our apartment for a while, enjoying a sense of newfound freedom.

When I enter, my daughter Molly and our new puppy dog run toward me and I pat and hug them. It's such a lovely moment of happiness that I wish I could be in it forever.

My husband, Tom, is at his desk, trying not to show any emotion. I hesitantly walk over to him, despite not wanting to. I give him a quick kiss regardless.

"What's up?" Tom must think I've given in.

I tell him that I missed him but that it doesn't mean that everything is okay between us. Oh, how I wish we could turn back time and be happily married again.

He notices that my shirt has become see-through from my wet bathing suit. Once upon a time it would have been a turn on, but instead, he looks at me in disgust.

Bold

I stand in the hallway outside our apartment, sea salt burning a small cut in my nose. I hold my shirt sleeve against it with my wrist, trying to sooth the sting—my handbag falls down around my elbow. My hair partly dry, stuck together in clumps like dreadlocks, tickles the back of my neck. Like a birthmark, the scent of ocean owns me. Smells like … freedom? Salt grains exfoliating pollution from my skin.

I open the door and Molly and our puppy come charging for me like bulls. Molly clutches the puppy's left ear. The puppy pants, her thick pink bouncy tongue hanging from the side of her mouth. I kneel down and hug them both at once. Drool splashes on my hand. I intend to scratch her behind her ears, and stroke Molly's hair, but my wires get crossed and I do the reverse. I wish the three of us could sit on the floor in the corridor all night—in a cocoon of unconditional love, freedom from the world, no responsibility, no ache, simple pleasure at its best.

My husband, Tom, is at his desk, blank-faced. I walk over to him, unsure of what to say, whether I want to say anything at all, or even if I want to be anywhere near him. I stand by his side. Don't utter a word. He doesn't look up. I bend down; semi-consciously give him a peck on the forehead.

"What's up?" Tom smirks as if I've given in. His voice snaps me back to reality.

"I missed you," I say, covering my bikini strap with my hair. "Doesn't mean I forgive you." I pull back. But I didn't miss him. I missed the idea of him; the impression of how we used to be.

He looks at my breasts through my damp shirt exposing blurred blue checks below. Once upon a time he would have cupped his hands over them, squeezed them, and nudged me toward the bedroom. But now ... he looks at them as if I'm violating some cultural indecent exposure law.

WHICH SENSES HAVE BEEN USED AND HOW?

Let me get you started ...

E.g., "I stand in the hallway outside our apartment, sea salt burning a small cut in my nose."

> see • feel • taste • smell

What can you see?
The apartment door and hallway

What can you feel?
Stinging inside nose, perhaps hesitant to go inside

What can you smell?
Sea salt, the beach, maybe wet hair

Read the BOLD example again. Isolate each sentence and identify what senses are being utilized, and how.

TRANSITION 8

Bleak

I'm at the Hilton Hotel standing outside the lecture hall door observing all the pompous people in this building. And I'm nervous about giving this presentation. So nervous that I feel like throwing up. I need to stop fidgeting and get my shit together.

It's time. I walk into the lecture hall and stand behind the podium. I feel sweaty and I'm worried my nerves are radiating into the crowd. I can just feel I'm going to make a fool of myself.

Everyone turns to face me and I begin to shake and choke on the words I practiced to introduce myself.

I don't think this is going to go very well.

Bold

At Hilton Hotel. Biting nails. Reciting presentation in head with the notes of guitar scales. Standing by lecture hall door, fingers twisted behind back, toes clenched in black baby-doll flats. Changed shoes in the car. Watching freshly dry-cleaned suits, worn by impassive breathing corpses, walk by. Black pencil skirts and dusty patent leather high-heeled shoes on Stepford Wife splendor. Clop. Clop. Clopping. Past me like old slides. Bus boys with crisp white shirts and ugly yellow ties. Upper-class ladies in frilly blouses who eat with their mouths closed at all times, and wait for the thirty-second mouthful before swallowing, and pat their lips with expensive linen napkins.

A piece of nail gets lodged between my front teeth. I try to pry it out, exposing my teeth like a growling dog, but failing because I have no nails left to pry it out with. Middle-aged man in navy blue tailored trousers and pink shirt with collar opened three buttons down, grins at me in a ridiculing manner. His gold chain glistens amidst his thick dark chest hair as he passes below a chandelier. *Rich bastard. Trying to follow trends.* I bring my arms down to my sides and close my mouth, pushing the nail through my teeth with my tongue. Grimacing within, I smile back with my lips pressed together so tight I imagine them turning white.

I'm nauseous. Not because of presentation nerves,

but because pink shirts make me want to vomit, for two reasons. One: they remind me of the time I was ten and put my white clothes in with the red bed sheets and mum pulled the heads off all my Barbie dolls as punishment. They also remind of when my husband got attacked by Greek rock venue mafia, and was left bleeding with a few knife gashes to his chest. White shirt stained with blood. Nothing serious. But what if it *had* been? I tried to scrub out the blood from his shirt by hand in the white porcelain bathroom sink. I'll never forget that feeling of infirmity spread from my feet, through my body, to the tip of my tongue. I had turned around and thrown up in the toilet bowl. Then continued to scrub, and had sung a stupid TV cheese jingle to distract myself from the overwhelming fear of what might happen next time.

It's time. I walk into the lecture hall and stand behind the podium. A bead of sweat tickles between my breasts. I want to scratch it. I grit my teeth trying to wane off the temptation, the air becoming a whirlwind of angst around my head. I cough into the microphone. Feedback. Feet shuffle. Voices murmur. Silence. A stray chuckle escapes from someone who was probably so preoccupied talking to the person next to them that they hadn't noticed I'd walked in.

Eyes focus on me as if I am an optometrist's letter chart. With shaking legs and a blank mind, I open my mouth to introduce myself, but words do not flee.

I'm screwed.

WHICH SENSES HAVE BEEN USED AND HOW?

Let me get you started ...

E.g., "At Hilton Hotel. Biting nails. Reciting presentation in head with the notes of guitar scales. Standing by lecture hall door, fingers twisted behind back, toes clenched in black baby-doll flats."

> see • feel • taste • hear

What can you see?
Interior of Hilton Hotel, a nervous woman

What can you feel?
Nervous tension, nails between teeth, twisted fingers, clenched toes

What can you taste?
Bitten nails

What can you hear?
Guitar scales, inner voice reciting presentation, perhaps voices of people walking around hotel

Read the BOLD example again. Isolate each sentence and identify what senses are being utilized, and how.

TRANSITION 9

Bleak

Though he attempted to be quiet and not wake up Linda, Sean didn't quite manage it. He farted when he sat on the edge of the bed. He sat in still silence, hoping the smell wouldn't spread through the sheets. But Linda woke up and giggled. Yup, she could smell it all right. Damn!

"You should go back to sleep. It's only nine o'clock," Sean said, standing up and looking at himself in the mirror.

"What time did we go to sleep?" Linda asked sleepily.

Sean stood up and looked out the window at a woman fetching her morning paper—an unappealing picture of domesticity.

"Not sure, but I came over around half four."

Linda rolled over and went back to sleep.

Sean went into Linda's messy and disorganized kitchen to make a coffee to discover there was no coffee maker in sight or even milk in the fridge. The sight of the packed cardboard boxes in front of him made him feel like he was moving forward in this relationship too fast.

He returned to the bedroom. "Babe, do you have a percolator?"

"No. Just use the hot tap, or boil some water in the small pot on the stove. Everything else is packed away," Linda said.

Sean looked out the window again. Now the woman was arguing with her inattentive husband over the Christmas tree delivery.

"It's a sign," he thought.

He couldn't go through with this.

Bold

Sean tried to sit on the edge of the bed without waking Linda. But failed miserably when his feet touched the carpet, and he accidentally let out a ripper of a fart. Damn! It bubbled behind his balls and sent dread through his chest. He stared at himself in the wardrobe mirror. *Maybe it's just loud because it's quiet in here.* He was afraid to move in case the smell spread through Linda's silky cotton sheets. His torso constricted; goose pimples formed around his nipples. Linda giggled and rubbed her eyes. *Shit. Can she smell it? I can smell it. Shit.* She nuzzled her face into her pillow and smudged makeup on it.

"Lovely," Linda croaked. "That's so much better than an alarm clock. Can you stay over during the week too?" She waved her hand in front of her nose.

"Sorry," Sean whispered.

"'S'not as bad as some I've experienced."

"You should go back to sleep. It's only nine o'clock," Sean said, standing and pulling on his boxers. He caught the reflection of his right bum cheek in the mirror. He had a huge hickey on it. *Are those teeth marks?*

"What time did we go to sleep?" Linda asked,

struggling to open her eyes and shadowing them with her hand. She lifted both legs into the air and hooked the duvet underneath her feet.

Sean stood up straight, motionless, staring out the window at the grey wet street. He could see a lady fetching the Sunday paper in her pajamas and gumboots. She ripped the plastic off, pulled out the Christmas catalogues, and threw the newspaper in the street bin.

"Not sure, but I came around half four."

Linda grunted in agreement, rolled over, and pulled the covers over her head.

Sean stumbled into the kitchen to put on a pot of coffee. But he couldn't find the percolator. Does she even have a percolator? Crumbs crunched under his bare feet and got stuck between his toes. The kitchen bench was bare, and the pantry full of herbs, self-rising flour, canned minestrone soup, Jacob's instant coffee, and old jars of strawberry jam and Vegemite. There was one jar of Marmite too, still sealed. That must be for emergencies.

The inside of the fridge looked like a hospital ward in the midst of a bomb scare. There was a plate of moldy blueberry pancakes, a box of Chinese noodles with chopsticks and a fork still in it, and a couple of cans of Malibu and Coke. No milk. In the dish rack there sat one bowl, one mug, one soup spoon, and one teaspoon.

Packed cardboard boxes, sitting dormant next to the kitchen table against the wall, stared at Sean. They teased him, rubbing the fast-approaching and ambivalent future into his face.

He returned to the bedroom and pulled the covers from Linda's face. She smiled with her eyes shut, like a child who'd secretly eaten all the cake, or drunk all the chocolate milk. Sean imagined her with a brown milky moustache.

"Babe, do you have a percolator?"

"No. Just use the hot tap, or boil some water in the small pot on the stove. Everything else is packed away," Linda said.

Sean didn't move. He looked out the window again. Now there was a truck delivering the woman a tree. She wore a heavy-looking coat over her pajamas this time. She pulled money out of her pocket and handed it to the delivery dude. Her husband ran out to help her drag the tree into the house. He was fully dressed and had his cell phone hooked between his ear and shoulder. The woman tripped, yelled something at her husband. He dropped the tree to the ground, held his finger up to his mouth to tell her to shoosh, and continued talking on his cell. She stamped her foot, threw her arms up in the air, and yelled something else before running back inside the house and slamming the front door.

The dread of another round of domesticity pricked at Sean's pores. Ugh.

WHICH SENSES HAVE BEEN USED AND HOW?

Let me get you started …

E.g. "Sean tried to sit on the edge of the bed without waking Linda. But failed miserably when his feet touched the carpet, and he accidentally let out a ripper of a fart."

> see • feel • hear • smell

What can you see?
A couple in bed, a carpeted bedroom

What can you feel?
Feet on carpet, warm vibration of fart, tentative, apologetic, embarrassed

What can you hear?
The fart, the quiet ruffle of bed sheets, the silence of morning

What can you smell?
The fart, and perhaps morning breath

Read the BOLD example again. Isolate each sentence and identify what senses are being utilized, and how.

TRANSITION 10

Bleak

Betty's drunk mother, Kay, who's passed out on the couch, looks like she's been starved to death and beaten up. Everyone in their suburban neighborhood must think they are good-for-nothing lowlifes. Not only is the place tiny, but you can tell it's a dump just by looking in the backyard.

Betty noisily passes Kay to get to the kitchen— frankly, she couldn't give a damn if she woke her up.

As Kay wheezes, Betty looks at her disgusting, foul-smelling mother's body and wonders if she'll ever get over the guilt of wishing her dead.

Bold

A bottle of Smirnoff lies on the floor, open, pleading next to Betty's mother, Kay, to wake up and take down its remaining drops with her morning cigarette. Kay's skeletal, feeble limbs are splayed in directions Betty recognizes as dead, bruised victims she's seen on Crime TV.

Their Australian suburban house is small—just slightly bigger than a caravan, but at least it doesn't have wheels—at least this means they're not quite "trailer trash" despite what others may think.

Betty passes Kay to go into the kitchenette, being sure to make as much noise as possible—frankly, she couldn't give a damn if she woke Kay up; she'd probably take that last sip of vodka and pass out again anyway.

Kay is wheezing a little, so she's still alive … so far. Betty wonders if she'll ever have to face the inevitable time when "passed out" will have evolved to "deceased." If she wishes for that day to come a lot sooner than fate has planned, what will follow? Devastation, or devastating relief? And if the latter, will guilt wheedle its way into every passing thought? Into her meals, dress, makeup, false nails?

A glob of drool vibrates in the corner of Kay's mouth

with every breath of air that struggles through her sticky cracked lips. Strands of stiff bleach-blonde hair, clumped together and matted below her ear, look petrified with dried saliva. Her fingers twitch. She has two black nails from when she jammed them in the hinge of the alcohol cabinet door. She groans. One eye opens. Betty stares right at it—a vibrant crystal blue bordered with a yellowy, bloodshot white.

WHICH SENSES HAVE BEEN USED AND HOW?

Let me get you started ...

E.g., "A bottle of Smirnoff lies on the floor, open, pleading for Betty's mother, Kay, to wake up and take down its remaining drops with her morning cigarette."

> see • feel • smell

What can you see?
A daughter looking at her alcoholic mother passed out on the floor

What can you feel?
Pity, or perhaps disgust

What can you smell?
Stale alcohol, stale cigarette smoke

Read the BOLD example again. Isolate each sentence and identify what senses are being utilized, and how.

TRANSITION 11

Bleak

I gaze up at the Acropolis in Athens, Greece, and I'm in awe of its ancient beauty.

Climbing to the top is difficult with my four-year-old daughter, Carla, in a wheelchair, but I manage to get her as far as the entrance—it's going to be a tough climb to the top as it's still quite hot for September. I'll need to find some help.

To my surprise, a little old lady offers the perfect solution. She gives me her scarf and fixes it around my neck like a big sling Carla can sit in.

I'm so appreciative of her help that I buy her something to eat and drink while she waits for us to return.

"Thanks so much. We won't be long," I say, nodding and smiling as we begin the climb.

Bold

I gaze at the Acropolis in Athens, Greece. The air, marinated with late Cretaceous limestone dust that once accommodated the feet of countless ancient civilians, caresses my cheeks. The grounds are bristled with tufts of dry and newly sprouting grass, and scattered with rock shavings, large, small, and just plain humungous. A thick film of beige dust has settled over the entire area, and I can't help but wonder, when I rub it between my fingers, whether I am touching the remains of a Greek God or Goddess.

Climbing to the top along the slippery cobblestone path proves to be difficult with my four-year-old daughter, Carla, in a wheelchair, but I manage to get her as far as the entrance, where the wide but bumpy road ends, and the stairway to heaven begins—a stairway I now wish Carla could walk up herself.

Shading my face with my right hand from the scorching early September sun, I scan for women tourists.

Perhaps someone has a child carrier Carla could fit in.

To my surprise, a short, plump old lady, wearing white sneakers and black widow's attire, taps me on the shoulder and says in English with a gentle Greek accent, "You want take child, I take wheelchair. I wait here, yes?" She removes her long black scarf from around her head and ties it around my neck and shoulder like a handbag. "This will help, *agapi mou*. She can sit, like chair. See?" She pushes her hands into the scarf to open it up.

Stunned by her kindness, all I immediately manage is an ebullient nod and smile.

"Thank you. Thank you, so much," I say, brainstorming how to demonstrate my appreciation. "Um, wait. One moment."

I dash to the kiosk and buy the lady a cheese pie and bottle of water. The lady takes a seat in Carla's wheelchair, and a hearty bite out of her pie, then holds it in the air as if toasting a glass of wine. Nodding and smacking her lips together, she says, "I wait here. You no worry. You *no* worry, *agapi mou*. Go. Go see brilliant structure." A flake of pastry drops off the pie and onto her chin as she takes another bite. A protruding skin-coloured mole secures it in position as she nods again in thanks.

"Thanks so much. We won't be long," I say, nodding and smiling in gratitude as we begin the daunting climb.

WHICH SENSES HAVE BEEN USED AND HOW?

Let me get you started ...

E.g., "I gaze at the Acropolis in Athens, Greece. The air, marinated with late Cretaceous limestone dust that once accommodated the feet of countless ancient civilians, caresses my cheeks."

> see • feel • hear • smell

What can you see?
The Acropolis, limestone, dust, and perhaps bare-footed ancient Greeks in Roman-style clothing

What can you feel?
A sense of magic, a soft breeze on my cheeks

What can you hear?
Perhaps background chatter, shuffling feet

What can you smell? The dust of dry rock, and perhaps Athens city pollution

Read the BOLD example again. Isolate each sentence and identify what senses are being utilized, and how.

NOW WHAT?

For the sake of practice, let's say that all the BOLD passages were written by you. Let's say that each one is a vignette (a **written snapshot**) that a literary journal wishes to publish, but in order for them to be published, they require you cut their length down by half.

In each WHICH SENSES HAVE BEEN USED AND HOW? section, I asked you to isolate each sentence of the BOLD passages and identify what senses are being utilized, and how. Refer to those lists and rewrite the BOLD passages using half as many words, but still using all the senses you listed.

When you're done, choose your best one and email it to me! I'd love to read it.

To email me your rewrites, please do so via the contact form on my website: **www.jessicabellauthor.com**

MAKE YOUR OWN INDEX OF SENSES

Feeling empowered? Why don't you create your own "Index of Senses" in the back of this book for future reference?

Check out the lined note-taking pages after the indexes for Book's #1 and #2. You can use this space.

The idea is to list the brief detail (i.e., *dust in air*) under their sense sub-headings (*see, feel, hear, smell, taste*), and direct yourself to the page of the transition in which it is portrayed (i.e., *The sun bled an orange glucose shard of light through the dusty blinds.*)

Don't forget to do it in alphabetical order! You might want to draft it up on a separate piece of paper before writing it in the book.

BONUS WRITING EXERCISES

1.

Step one: Where are you sitting right now? Look around you and make a list of everything you see, hear, smell, feel.

Step two: Write a scene using every single item on your list. There is no word limit. Just write until it's finished.

2.

Step one: Think of a place abroad you have visited. What is the first thing that comes to mind about it that inspires you? Tell your reader why it inspires you in 250 to 500 words, as if in a journal. If you haven't travelled abroad, choose something from your home town.

Step two: Transform your paragraph into a "showing" scene. Write no more than 1000 words.

3.

You are going to write a short scene between two characters, A and B (any gender and age). A dislikes B, but B has a romantic crush on A. At the end of the scene they should both have the opposite opinion of one another: B begins to dislike A, and A begins to crush on B. We should be able to witness the transition from beginning to end. But there's a catch. You must write from the point of view of ONE character only. Use 3rd person limited, past tense. Use at least three similes/metaphors in your scene. It can be as many words as you wish.

4.

Rewrite the scene from Exercise #3 from the other character's point of view. Use 1st person, present tense.

5.

Think about the person you are in love with. If you are not in love with anyone, think of someone you love unconditionally, such as a parent, sibling, child, or pet. Write a scene between you and this person/pet that illustrates the extent of your love through action. You must not use the word love at all, any synonyms of love, or any declaration of your feelings. The reader must **see** that you love this person from the way you behave. Avoid clichés such as cheek stroking, and looking longingly into one's eyes. Use at least one simile/metaphor in your scene that relates to smell. Use 1st person, past tense. Write no more than 1000 words.

6.

Repeat Exercise #5. Replace the feeling of love with a feeling of disappointment. Use at least one simile/metaphor in your scene that relates to taste. Use 3rd person, present tense.

7.

Write a one-page memoir from the point of view of an inanimate object. Don't think about it too long. Just choose the first object that comes to mind. Think about its function. Does it need another object, or a living being, in order to efficiently serve its purpose? If so, what kind of relationship would this object have with this other object/living being, and how would that relationship shape the object's life? Try to avoid giving the object supernatural abilities. Be as realistic with it as possible, but be sure to give it a "voice."

8.

Step one: Watch the first ten minutes of your favourite movie (or until the opening scene comes to a natural end). If there is dialogue, write it down. If not, describe what is happening.

Note: Do not do this exercise with a movie that has been adapted from a novel you have read.

Step two: Dissect the behaviour and actions of the actors, and/or the appearance and atmosphere of the setting. Write the first ten minutes of the movie as if it were the opening chapter of a novel.

9.

Step one: Listen to a song that makes you emotional. In point form, write down how it makes you feel, the memories it evokes, and anything non-specific that comes to mind.

Step two: Use your list to adapt the song into a vignette. You do not have to directly use every single thing on your list. It is there for inspiration. Listen to the song as many times as necessary. Avoid using actual lyrics from the song. You might like to submit your finished piece to a literary journal (like mine!) and you do not want to infringe copyright.

10.

Step one: Grab your favourite novel. Turn to a random page. Read through it as many times as necessary to extract the emotions and senses it uses. List them.

Step two: Are there any similes and/or metaphors used? If so, write down what they illustrate.

Step three: Put the novel away. Use the information you listed in steps one and two to write your own scene. Use the same tense and point of view that is used in the novel, however, your new scene should not resemble the genre, theme(s), or plot of the novel in any way.

11.

Step one: Divide a piece of paper into three columns. Write each letter of the alphabet vertically in the first column. Think of an emotion/feeling that begins with each letter. Write them next to the letters in the second column.

Step two: For each emotion/feeling you have written down, think of a certain behaviour and/ or expression that illustrates it. Write them in the third column.

Step three: On a separate piece of paper, divide the behaviours/expressions into groups: negative, positive, indifferent.

Step four: Use the behaviours/expressions you have written in a piece of writing. Do not use them just for the sake of using them. Make sure your writing remains realistic, and the behaviours/ expressions are warranted. If you cannot add any more to your piece without jeopardizing its authenticity, start a new one. Continue until you have used every single behaviour/expression in a piece of writing.

12.

Step one: If you're a poetry fan, find your favourite poem. If you're not a poetry fan, feel free to choose one of mine. Read it through once. Write down the feelings it evokes.

Step two: Read through the poem again. What is it about? Note down your thoughts. Do not be afraid of getting wrong answers. There is no such thing as a wrong answer here. This exercise is designed to purely spark your imagination.

Step three: Read through the poem again, more

slowly, focusing on one line at a time. Identify the imagery each line evokes, and the deeper emotions related to this imagery. Has any kind of symbolism been used to illustrate this emotion? If so, what? Is there a prominent theme? Make notes. If you're drawing a blank, which might be the case if you have never read poetry before, choose a word from each line, and play a word-association game with yourself. This might help trigger some ideas.

Step four: Read the poem again. Is there any sort of narrative (does it tell a story)? If there is no narrative, create one of your own based on the information you have written down in steps one to three. Now adapt this poem into a short story or vignette.

Note: *If you use one of my poems for this exercise, please email your piece to me. I'd love to see what you've come up with! You never know, maybe I'll like it so much that I'll publish it in Vine Leaves Literary Journal.*

13.

Step one: Choose your favourite television series and write out the dialogue for as much of one episode as you can. Not from memory! Watch the episode and pause the video to write it down.

Step two: Read through the dialogue while simultaneously watching the episode again. Identify the instances of subtext (the meaning beneath the dialogue; what the speaker really means, but doesn't say). A character's behaviour will always embody clues.

Step three: Refer to your notes from step two to write a completely different scene using the subtext you identified.

14.

Choose three random words, preferably a noun, an adjective, and a verb. Use them to write the first line of your next project. Make it as concise as possible. Avoid run-on sentences. Implement an element of intrigue. Maybe it will become the first line of your next novel!

15.

Step one: Grab a newspaper (or your iPad!) and open to a random page. Read the first headline that catches your eye. Write it down. Do not read the article.

Step two: Write a fictional article with the same headline. If you know the real story from the news, choose another one. If you know every single story that has been in the news lately, make up your own headline.

Step three: Use the people mentioned in your article, and the things that happened to them, or the events they are associated with, to write a short story or vignette. Try to "show" as much as possible.

INDEX OF ATTRIBUTES (Book #1)

INDEX OF ADVERBS (Book #2)

INDEX OF CLICHÉS (Book #2)

If you found *Writing in a Nutshell* helpful, please do me the honour of leaving a review at the retailer's website from which you purchased this book. If you are a member of Goodreads.com, you will find this book there, too. Your reviews and support help me immensely, and are very much appreciated!

Jessica Bell

CPSIA information can be obtained at www.ICGtesting.com
Printed in the USA
BVOW05s0030140314

347600BV00007B/82/P

9 780987 593177